AN EASY-READ COMMUNITY BOOK

WHY DO WE HAVE RULES?

BY CAROLINE ARNOLD

PHOTOGRAPHS BY GINGER GILES

Franklin Watts
New York/London/Toronto/Sydney
1983

Cover photograph courtesy of Cass R. Sandak

Special thanks are due the following individuals and organizations whose cooperation made the photographs possible:

Linda Biddle, Kelley Elementary School, Moore, Okla.; Patrick Gavin; Judie Mills; Jeanne Vestal; Lydia Stein; Gregory Gardner; Jeff Horton.

Photographs courtesy of: pages 7, 13, and 15, Frank Sloan; pages 16, 18, and 19, United Press International, Inc.; page 20, Nancy Hays from Monkmeyer Press Photo Service; page 21, Mimi Forsyth from Monkmeyer Press Photo Service; page 25, ABC News; page 27, New York Post Office; page 30, United Nations.

R.L. 2.6 Spache Revised Formula

Library of Congress Cataloging in Publication Data

Arnold, Caroline.
Why do we have rules?

(An Easy-read community book)
Summary: A basic discussion of the need for
rules in society and of how our government
is formed, chosen, and used.
1. State, The—Juvenile literature.
2. Civics—Juvenile literature. [1. Civics.
2. United States—Politics and government
I. Giles, Ginger, ill. II. Title. III. Series.
JC325.A67 1983   320.4   82-17535
ISBN 0-531-04509-9

CONTENTS

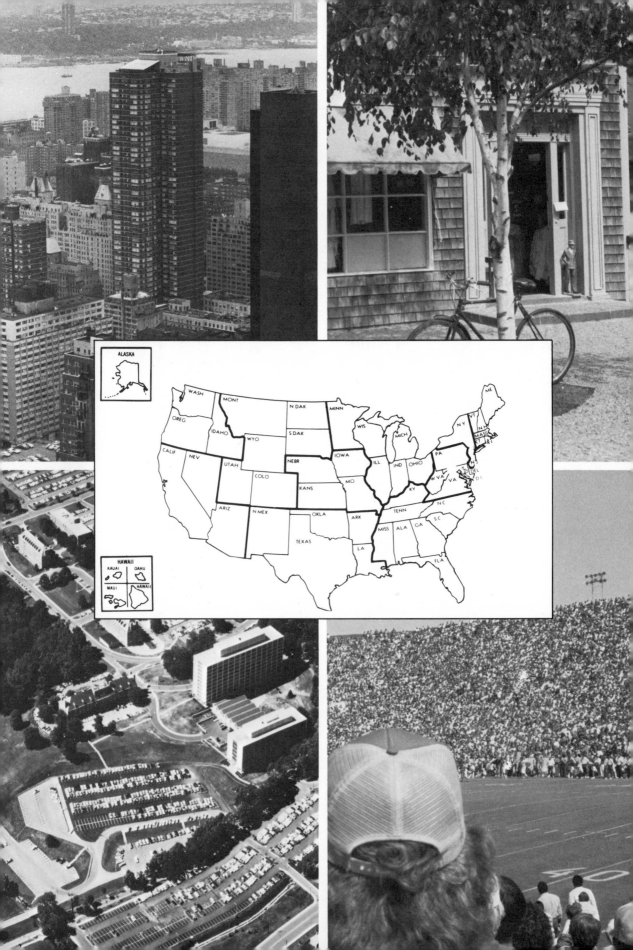

Where Do You Live?

Our country is the United States of America. It is one of the largest countries in the world. There are over 200 million people who live here.

The United States of America is divided into fifty parts. Each part is called a state. Some states are very big. Some are very small. Some are in between. What state do you live in?

Every state is divided into smaller
parts. Each part is usually called a county.
Do you know the name of the county
you live in?

Each county is usually divided into several towns or townships.

Every state also has big cities and towns within some counties.

A map can help you find out where people live in your state.

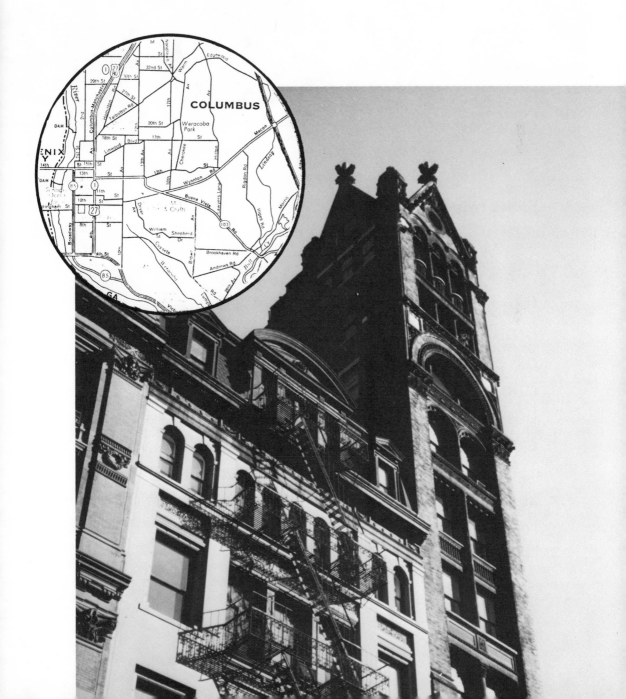

Everyone Needs Rules

When people live together they need to have rules. Rules help keep things in order. Rules help solve problems if people do not agree. We have rules for health and safety. We have rules about schools, property, and business. We also have rules that promise each person's freedom.

We have rules at home, at work, and at school. In your school there may be rules for your class. There may also be rules for the whole school.

Rules help you behave in the halls and in class.

Rules help keep the school safe and clean.

Rules help make your school a good place for everyone.

Rules help you play fairly in the playground.

We all follow rules every day in our
communities.

Every community has traffic rules.
Can you imagine what would happen if
there were no stop signs? Or what would
happen if cars could drive at any speed?

Every community has rules to help keep it clean. Most communities provide places to get rid of trash. They try to keep their water and air clean, too.

Communities also have rules that say that it is wrong to rob or hurt other people.

Can you think of some rules that help make your community a good place to live?

What Is Government?

When people get together to make rules, they form a government. Your school may have a student government, often called a student council. You may help to choose one person in your class to be part of the student council. The student council helps to plan school events and to make some of the rules for the whole school.

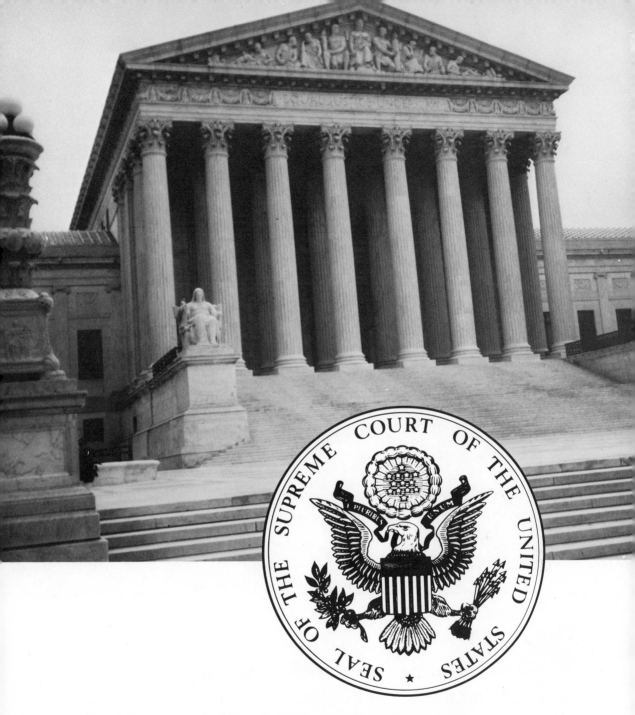

We also have governments for our
cities, counties, states, and our country.
They make the rules for the people who
live there.

Each city and town makes its own rules. The government offices are in the city hall or the town hall.

Counties make rules, too. Usually the government offices of the county are in the largest town in the county. It is called the county seat.

State rules are made by the governments of each state. Each state has a capital city for its government offices. What is the capital of your state?

We also need rules for our whole country. They are made by the government of the United States. The main offices of the government of the United States are in Washington, D.C. Washington, D.C., is the capital of our country.

Who Is in Charge?

In the United States, there are three main parts of government. One part makes the rules. Another part makes sure the rules are followed. A third part decides exactly what the rules mean.

Every government needs leaders. Leaders make sure that everybody follows the rules.

The head of the government of our country is the president. The head of each state is the governor. The head of most cities and towns is the mayor. Some counties and towns have a small group of people in charge instead of just one person.

Who Makes the Rules?

Some rules are the same for
everyone. Other rules are just for one
state, county, or town.

The rules for our country are called
laws. They are made by people called
senators and representatives. They meet
together in Washington, D.C., in the
Congress.

Each state has two senators. Big states have many representatives. Small states have just a few. In the Congress, senators and representatives write the laws and vote on them.

State senators and representatives make laws for the states. They meet in state legislatures.

In some towns everyone who lives in the town is part of the government. When they need to decide something they have a town meeting. Each person helps to make the laws.

In large towns and counties there are too many people to have a town meeting. Then they choose a few people to make the laws for them.

In the county there may be a board of supervisors.

In a city it may be the city council.

Do you know who represents you in your town or city government?

Deciding Right and Wrong

Sometimes two people cannot agree about what a law means. Then a judge must decide what is right.

Sometimes a person breaks a law. Then a judge must decide how the person should be punished.

In our country each person has the right to a fair trial. That means that no one can be punished until it is proved that he or she broke the law.

Sometimes a jury helps a judge. A
jury is a group of twelve people. They
listen to all the facts. Then the judge
helps them decide whether or not the
law has been broken.

Judges and juries make their
decisions in courts. We have courts for
our country, states, counties, and towns.

We Choose Our Government

The government of the United States is a democracy. In a democracy each person helps to decide what the rules will be. We do this by voting. Citizens who are eighteen or older can vote.

You may have seen people going to vote on Election Day.

In some places people vote on voting machines. Sometimes people write their votes on a piece of paper.

Sometimes people vote to try to make a new law. If enough people vote for it then it becomes a law.

Sometimes we vote for people to make the rules for us. We try to choose people who will make rules that are fair. The person who gets the most votes wins.

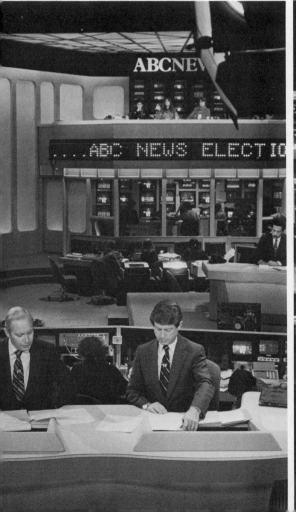

We vote for people to work in many parts of the government. These people then sometimes choose other people to help them.

Sometimes we vote for people to be on the school board of our community. The school board then hires people to build schools. They hire teachers and principals to work in the schools, too.

Many people work for the government. Mail carriers, street cleaners, and the police are some of them. The government needs secretaries, clerks, and truck drivers, too.

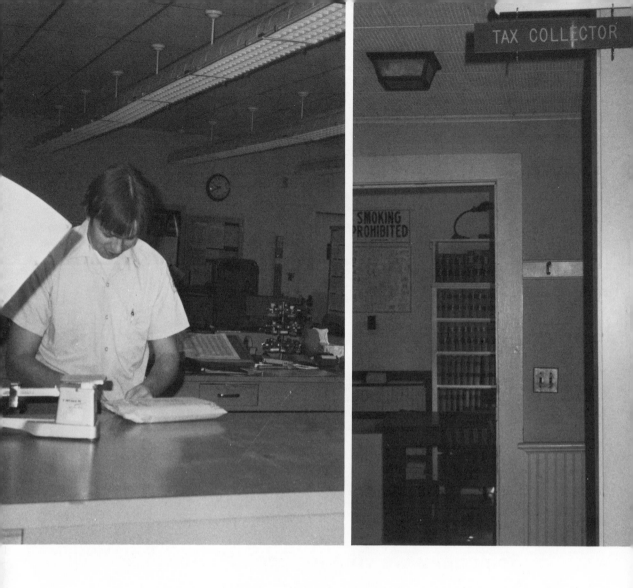

Who Pays for Government?

People who work for the government need to be paid for their jobs just like other people. The government also needs money to pay for roads, schools, and other things the community needs.

The government gets money from taxes. A tax is money that must be paid to the government by people. Tax on money that a person earns is called income tax. Tax on things you buy is called sales tax. People who own houses and land must pay property taxes.

Who Defends Us?

Each country in the world has its own rules. In our country we all follow the rules of the United States.

In the United Nations people from many countries meet together. They try to agree on rules that people in all countries can follow.

Sometimes two countries do not agree about something. The United Nations may try to help them come to a peaceful solution. But sometimes two countries cannot solve their problems peacefully. Then they have a war.

We do not like to have wars. In wars people get hurt or killed and property is destroyed.

Wars are fought on land, on sea, and in the air.

We have people in the army, navy, marines and the air force. They will fight for our country if they need to.

We feel safe because we know they are there to defend us.

Rules are important. They help keep order in our homes, schools, and communities. They help make them a better place to live.